MAXFIELD PARRISH

MW01077388

A Book of Postcards

Pomegranate Artbooks, San Francisco

Pomegranate Artbooks
Box 808022
Petaluma, CA 94975

ISBN 0-87654-942-3
Pomegranate Catalog No. A593

Pomegranate publishes several other postcard collections on many different subjects.
Please write to the publisher for more information.

Cover design by Riba Taylor
Printed in Korea

Maxfield Parrish (1870-1966) was among the best-known and most prolific professional artists of his time, especially during the early part of this century. In one form or another—as magazine and book illustrations, calendars, posters, art prints and so on—his paintings entered count-less homes and made his name a household word. Adver-tisers prized Parrish's works as effective vehicles for selling products ranging from seeds to chocolates and perfume. Writers and publishers knew that illustrations by Parrish could only enhance their texts. And art reproduction houses found a never-before-imagined market for Parrish posters. Maxfield Parrish became the most reproduced American artist, and his paintings became American icons, as familiar and comforting as trusted friends.

This selection of 30 full-color reproductions of Parrish paintings concisely demonstrates his exquisite and exacting technique, his unique, vibrant palette and his keen ability to portray the most romantic of atmospheres. In studying this collection, we become immersed in a world of magic, light and dreams, where we can find both solace and adventure.

MAXFIELD PARRISH
The Canyon, 1923
Oil on masonite, 19$\frac{1}{2}$ x 15 in.
Original version published as cover for *Life*,
March 1923; this altered version published
as a reproduction by House of Art, September 1924

Pomegranate, Box 808022, Petaluma, CA 94975

MAXFIELD PARRISH
Air Castles
Cover for *The Ladies' Home Journal,*
September 1904

Pomegranate, Box 808022, Petaluma, CA 94975

MAXFIELD PARRISH
Ecstasy, 1929
Oil on masonite, 36 x 24 in.
1930 calendar for General Electric
Edison Mazda Lamps

Pomegranate, Box 808022, Petaluma, CA 94975

MAXFIELD PARRISH

The Lantern Bearers, 1908
Oil on canvas, 40 x 32 in.
Illustration for *Collier's*, December 10, 1910

Pomegranate, Box 808022, Petaluma, CA 94975

MAXFIELD PARRISH
The Lute Players, 1922
Oil on canvas, 6 ft. 11 in. x 4 ft. 11 in.
Mural for Eastman Theater, Rochester, New York;
released as a color print by House of Art, 1924

Pomegranate, Box 808022, Petaluma, CA 94975

MAXFIELD PARRISH

Griselda, 1909
Oil on canvas laid down on masonite, 38 x 81 in.
Illustration for Florence Wilkinson's "Seven Green
Pools at Cintra," published by *Century Magazine*,
August 1910; this version renamed *Griselda* by
Parrish after he painted out the original background

Pomegranate, Box 808022, Petaluma, CA 94975

MAXFIELD PARRISH
Hilltop, 1926
Oil on masonite, 35$\frac{1}{8}$ x 21$\frac{3}{4}$ in.

Pomegranate, Box 808022, Petaluma, CA 94975

MAXFIELD PARRISH
Gulnare of the Sea (detail), 1906
Frontispiece for "Arabian Nights X," published
by *Collier's*, August 3, 1907; also in *The Arabian
Nights: Their Best-Known Tales*, edited by Kate
Douglas Wiggin and Nora A. Smith, Charles
Scribner's Sons, 1909

Pomegranate, Box 808022, Petaluma, CA 94975

MAXFIELD PARRISH
Enchantment (Cinderella), 1914
Oil on masonite, 32 x 26 in.
Cover for *Harper's Bazar,* March 1914; 1926
calendar for General Electric Edison Mazda Lamps

Pomegranate, Box 808022, Petaluma, CA 94975

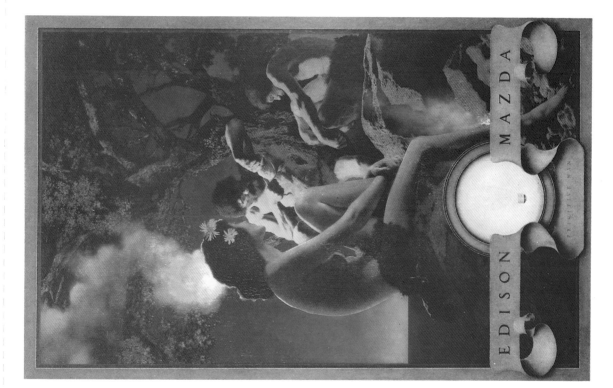

MAXFIELD PARRISH
Primitive Man, 1920
Oil on masonite
1921 calendar for General Electric
Edison Mazda Lamps

Pomegranate, Box 808022, Petaluma, CA 94975

EDISON MAZDA LAMPS · USE MAZDA LAMPS

GOLDEN HOURS

MAXFIELD PARRISH
Golden Hours (Autumn), 1927
Oil on masonite
1929 calendar for General Electric
Edison Mazda Lamps

Pomegranate, Box 808022, Petaluma, CA 94975

MAXFIELD PARRISH
Venetian Lamplighter, 1922
Oil on masonite, 28 x 18 in.
1924 calendar for General Electric
Edison Mazda Lamps

Pomegranate, Box 808022, Petaluma, CA 94975

MAXFIELD PARRISH
Puss-in-Boots, 1914
Cover for *Hearst's Magazine,* May 1914

Pomegranate, Box 808022, Petaluma, CA 94975

OLD KING COLE

MAXFIELD PARRISH

Old King Cole (detail, center panel), 1906
Oil on canvas, 8 ft. x 30 ft.
Mural for Hotel Knickerbocker, New York City;
now located at St. Regis Hotel, New York City

Pomegranate, Box 808022, Petaluma, CA 94975

MAXFIELD PARRISH
Reveries (*The Fountain*), 1926
Oil on masonite, c. 35 x 22 in.
1927 calendar for General Electric
Edison Mazda Lamps

Pomegranate, Box 808022, Petaluma, CA 94975

MAXFIELD PARRISH
The Young King of the Black Isles, 1906
Frontispiece for "Arabian Nights VIII," published
by *Collier's*, May 18, 1907; also in *The Arabian
Nights: Their Best-Known Tales*, edited by Kate
Douglas Wiggin and Nora A. Smith, Charles
Scribner's Sons, 1909

Pomegranate, Box 808022, Petaluma, CA 94975

MAXFIELD PARRISH
The Lamp Seller of Bagdad
Oil on masonite
1923 calendar for General Electric
Edison Mazda Lamps

Pomegranate, Box 808022, Petaluma, CA 94975

MAXFIELD PARRISH
Graduation painting, 1897
For the Pennsylvania Academy of Fine Arts

Pomegranate, Box 808022, Petaluma, CA 94975

MAXFIELD PARRISH

The History of Prince Codadad and His Brothers
Frontispiece for "Arabian Nights II," published by
Collier's, September 1, 1906; also in *The Arabian
Nights: Their Best-Known Tales*, edited by Kate
Douglas Wiggin and Nora A. Smith, Charles
Scribner's Sons, 1909

Pomegranate, Box 808022, Petaluma, CA 94975

MAXFIELD PARRISH
Moonlight, 1932
Oil on masonite, c. 32 x 23 in.
1934 calendar for General Electric
Edison Mazda Lamps

Pomegranate, Box 808022, Petaluma, CA 94975

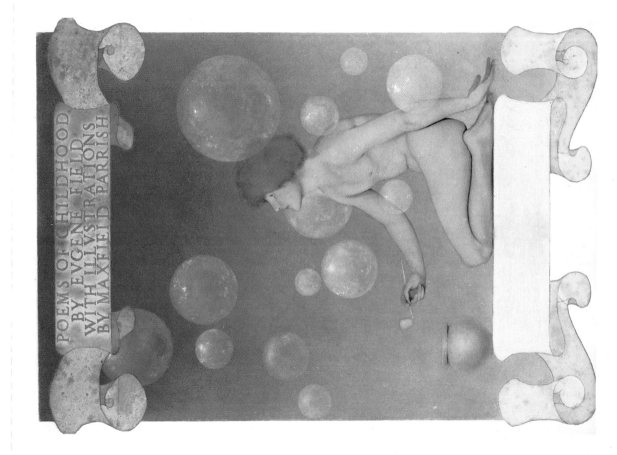

POEMS OF CHILDHOOD
BY EVGENE FIELD
WITH ILLVSTRATIONS
BY MAXFIELD PARRISH

MAXFIELD PARRISH
Title page from *Poems of Childhood* by Eugene Field,
Charles Scribner's Sons, 1904

Pomegranate, Box 808022, Petaluma, CA 94975

MAXFIELD PARRISH
Dream Light, 1924
Oil on masonite
1925 calendar for General Electric
Edison Mazda Lamps

Pomegranate, Box 808022, Petaluma, CA 94975

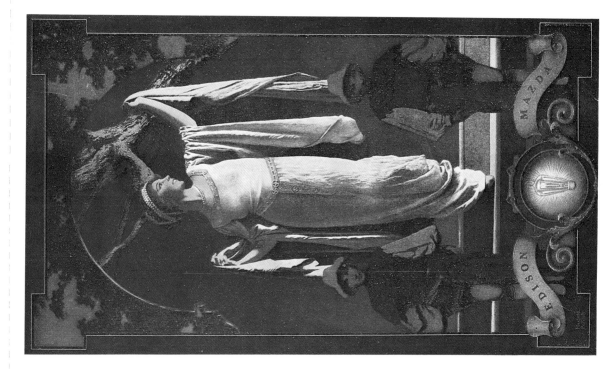

MAXFIELD PARRISH
Spirit of the Night
Oil on panel
1919 calendar for General Electric
Edison Mazda Lamps

Pomegranate, Box 808022, Petaluma, CA 94975

THE LADIES' HOME JOURNAL

CHRISTMAS 1912

FIFTEEN CENTS · THE CURTIS PUBLISHING COMPANY PHILADELPHIA

MAXFIELD PARRISH
Cover of *The Ladies' Home Journal*, Christmas 1912

Pomegranate, Box 808022, Petaluma, CA 94975

MAXFIELD PARRISH
The Spirit of Transportation, 1920
Competition piece for the Clark Equipment Company

Pomegranate, Box 808022, Petaluma, CA 94975

MAXFIELD PARRISH

A Venetian Night's Entertainment, 1903
Oil, 17 x 11½ in.
Frontispiece for Edith Wharton's "A Venetian Night's
Entertainment," published by *Scribner's Magazine,*
December 1903

Pomegranate, Box 808022, Petaluma, CA 94975

MAXFIELD PARRISH
Sunrise, 1931
Oil on masonite, 31¾ x 22½ in.
1933 calendar for General Electric
Edison Mazda Lamps

Pomegranate, Box 808022, Petaluma, CA 94975

MAXFIELD PARRISH
The Cardinal Archbishop, 1901
Frontispiece for Arthur Cosslett Smith's
"The Turquoise Cup," published by *Scribner's
Magazine*, December 1901; also frontispiece for
The Turquoise Cup, by Arthur Cosslett Smith,
Charles Scribner's Sons, 1903

Pomegranate, Box 808022, Petaluma, CA 94975

MAXFIELD PARRISH
Solitude, 1931
Oil on masonite
1932 calendar for General Electric
Edison Mazda Lamps

Pomegranate, Box 808022, Petaluma, CA 94975

MAXFIELD PARRISH

The Dinkey-Bird
Illustration for *Poems of Childhood* by Eugene Field,
Charles Scribner's Sons, 1904

Pomegranate, Box 808022, Petaluma, CA 94975